Belinda H. McKenzie
Edzell, Scotland
Aug 1981

TAKE ONE GLEN

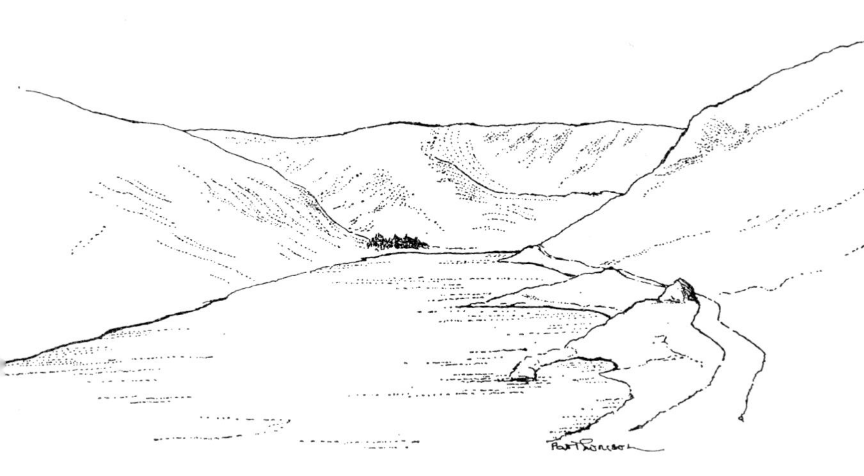

Loch Lee

Take One Glen

Compiled and illustrated
by

PAT THOMSON

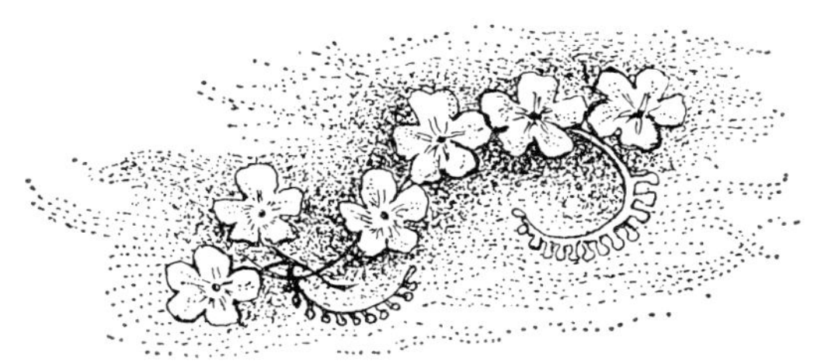

MONTROSE:
STANDARD PRESS
1977

First published 1973
Second edition 1977

Printed at the Standard Press
Montrose, Scotland.

To Seonaid and Lindsay — and Michael
whose every encouragement made
this book possible.

Bluebell

Contents

CONTENTS

Foreword

GLENESK, "the glen of glens", and inspiration of poets and writers from Alexander Ross to those of more recent times like John Angus, Violet Jacob and Helen Cruickshank, is not only noted for its wonderful variation of scenic beauty, but also for the hospitality meted out to friend and stranger alike.

The phrases "Come in, sit doon, and I'll pit the kettle on" and "... but ye canna gang awa withoot haen a cup o' something", or "Sit doon and gie's yer crack", summarise this deep basic kindliness and generosity. The feeling that emanates from this attitude is that people rather than time-tables are the things that really matter.

The recipes in this book show a cross-section of glen fare and, I hope, will also show part of the essence of glen life which makes it a place — perhaps a haven — that people return to time and time again.

My grateful thanks to all those ladies who contributed so freely to this collection and made the book possible.

October 1973. PAT THOMSON.

Looking up Glenesk
towards Maskeldie and Hunt Hill

The Glen

GLENESK IS a lovely glen, all the way from the low foothills of the Grampian range at Edzell to the wild grandeur of Glenmark and Maskeldie in its upper reaches, and each small glen that leads off from the main valley has its own individual beauty too.

Glenmark is dominated first by the ruggedness of Gilfumman, a vast rocky outcrop of a hill, and then by the high slopes of Mount Keen beyond. This is a favourite place for hill-walkers. The many cairns dotted around its slopes testify to the number who have climbed that way to Deeside. Not many people seem able to pass a cairn of stones and resist the temptation to add one more to the pile!

As you follow the Burn of Mark round Craig o' Doune, you pass some ruinous habitations before reaching the Falls of Mark. There the water has carved a spectacular chasm out of the solid rock, and the leap and roar can be heard a long way off.

Over the hill to the west lies Glenlee, with Unich beyond. Here bulldozers have scarred the hillside to provide tracks for Land Rovers, where before there were only bridle paths to the shooting butts. But apart from these and the Stables of Lee and the now ruinous Stables of Unich there is little evidence of the hand of man in these parts. The deer forest has changed little through the centuries. There is still a feeling of timelessness in the heather and bog and the swift-flowing burns.

The waters of Lee and Unich meet on the valley floor, the Unich thundering over rocks in two spectacular falls to join its sister burn, before meandering quietly down to Loch Lee. High above this loch lies another, the small but beautiful Carlochie, just below the towering peak of Maskeldie. From the foot of Loch Lee runs the Esk valley proper and the river adopts that name half-a-mile downstream, where the Mark joins the Lee in the fields below Invermark Castle.

The character of the countryside is changing now. The fields and parks of farms fringe the river banks. But the hills are never far away. A detour up the Branny Burn or Glen Effock leads again to the high places, undisturbed except for the calls of birds and sheep.

On the banks of the River Tarf, not far from where it runs into the Esk, is the small village of Tarfside, with a school, a post office, a smattering of houses and a masonic hall which is the hub of social life in the glen. Behind Tarfside lie Glentennet and the path to Aboyne, while across-river is the district of Arsallary, a wide rolling valley which bears mute testimony to a past life that can never return. Here the main impact lies not only in the lovely view but in the density of ruins scattered around. There are many ruined homesteads elsewhere in the Glen, but none conveys with such force the impression of a lost way of life. Perhaps it is the vision of a dispersed community — rather than of a family departed from a dwelling — that gives the scene such an air of poignancy.

The river and road run more or less parallel, down through a now widening valley, and the hills are still high on each side though more softly undulating. Adding to the contrast between the lower slopes and the rugged uplands are the natural woodlands, predominantly birch. The river banks, however, are lined with alder, known locally as "arran", which is probably a corruption of the Gaelic name for the species.

We are now near the foot of the glen, and the Esk is passing through fields where it has obviously meandered a great deal in geological times. This has long been a favourite haunt of painters and photographers, a scene which makes you stop and admire, as the birk woods suddenly open out to the panorama beyond. We are close to the Rocks of Solitude.

Rowan Hill

In Olden Times

THERE IS plenty of evidence "lyin' aboot" that the history of the Glen goes back to very early man. A short cist on top of Cairn Robie testifies to the fact that some three thousand five hundred years ago nomadic man was wandering there in search of pasture for his beasts. And if one's interest lies in the realms of geological time rather than human history, in those days too it was rather special. Lying close to the Highland Fault, it has long been a source of interest to geologists.

The valley floor in early times was mainly marshland and agriculture was carried out much higher up the hillsides. At Keenie, Glen Effock, the Rowan and elsewhere you can still see the ridge-and-furrow scars of run-rig, now overgrown with heather but still standing out clearly in a play of light and shade or when snow covers the ground.

The Rowan Hill has a superabundance of history scattered across its slopes. Here the difficulty lies not in seeing — there is so much to see — but in trying to interpret what is there. The top of the hill is dominated by the Tower, a cone-shaped monument raised last century by the then Earl of Dalhousie in memory of his family. And many who climb the hill from sheer curiosity, to see close at hand what the Tower is like, end up spell-bound by the view — down the Glen towards the Hill of Wirren, across to Glentennet and the Baillies, across on the opposite side to Glen Effock, and up towards Glenmark and Loch Lee. All these can be seen by merely moving a few feet at a time.

Hut circles, cairns and old pathways are among the many remains on the lower slopes of the Rowan. The largest circle is forty feet in diameter and some of the others are thought to be the remains of shieling sites that herdsmen used when they took their cattle out for summer pasture in medieval times.

Invermark Castle
(once owned by the Lindsays)

Legends have grown up around the cairns. For many generations it was firmly believed that the hill got its name because Robert the Bruce rallied his troops with the cry "Row-in! Row-in!" when he fought the Red Comyn here. The cairns themselves were reputed to be the graves of fallen warriors. But now this tale carries no credibility. Though Bruce was in the area, he was so ill that he had to be transported on a litter and was therefore avoiding any kind of confrontation.

Some of the cairns are field clearance, or "consumption dykes" as they are called, but others are burial cairns. They have all been opened and explored during the centuries. One was found in the nineteenth century to contain bodies buried in a crouched position, which would seem to indicate that they were a Bronze Age people. No one can be sure whether those primitive tombs accumulated over a period of time or whether there was a scourge of some sort, whether war or pestilence, which resulted in mass burial. So much remains uncharted in this period of prehistory that one can only look and surmise.

A stone by the side of the old road from Tarfside to Westbank has a cross carved deep into its face. This, like the cairns, is supposed to have associations with Robert the Bruce. But the cross may well date from a much earlier period, perhaps even from the time when St Drostan and his monks settled in Glenesk to spread the Gospel. He arrived in these parts about 600 A.D. and his name has passed into the folklore and place names of the Glen. The present-day Episcopal Church in Tarfside is St Drostan's and there are also — by affectionate corruption of his name — Droustie's Meadow and Droustie's Well. In time past an inn also bore his name. The char fish found today in Loch Lee and in Easter and Wester Carlochie (Carlochie means 'char loch') are said to have been introduced by Drostan and his monks. Certainly they are a species uncommon in the area but whether they were in fact introduced by him is by no means certain. They may have survived the Ice Age in this isolated pocket.

In medieval times the glen was owned by the Lindsay family. It is well nigh impossible to read Scottish history without the name of Lindsay featuring somewhere in the saga of past events.

Their sphere of influence was wide from early times. Even Elcho Nunnery, which survived up to the Reformation near where the Tay and Earn meet, was founded in the thirteenth century by a Glenesk Lindsay.

The Lindsays did nothing by half. For good or ill, they tackled fate with an uncommon passion and drive. Near the foot of the Glen you can see the sparse remains of Auchmull Castle, where one of them took refuge after a fatal brawl in Edinburgh. Most of the stones of this castle have since been incorporated into the nearby farm buildings. And in the grounds of Edzell Castle you can see the beautiful Pleasance which was created by that laird's father, David Lindsay. Cultured and well travelled, he bequeathed to posterity a love of beauty and the fine things in life. He had little else to bequeath. His furtherance of the arts brought him over the edge of penury.

Close to the Cross Stone, on the old road by the Rowan, is the site of an Episcopal chapel which saw ruination in the turbulent days of the Jacobite cause. Those were the days when the majority of the glensfolk were Episcopalian, with a strong allegiance to "the king across the water", and feeling ran high when their minister, a Mr Rose, was arrested and imprisoned at the start of the '45 Rebellion. What angered them most was the suspicion that his arrest had been engineered by his Presbyterian counterpart, Scott, the minister of Lochlee Kirk, a bitter enemy of the Episcopal Church. So much for "brethren in Christ", in the days when shades of opinion ran high and emotions deep. Scott was thrown from his horse and killed a few years later, while he was passing the 'Piscy church, and folk were not slow to point out that "That was the price o' him!"

The church on the Rowan was razed to the ground in the aftermath of the '45, when the Glen was visited by Government troops, the hated Argyll Highlanders. They were ruthless in their task of mopping-up. Though Glenesk has a long tradition of hospitality and kindliness, those troops found no welcome and the hatred nurtured towards them took a long time to fade away. As a child I once heard a tale of a very dead Redcoat being fished out of a small pool near Tarfside. But whether this was wishful thinking or actual fact I never discovered.

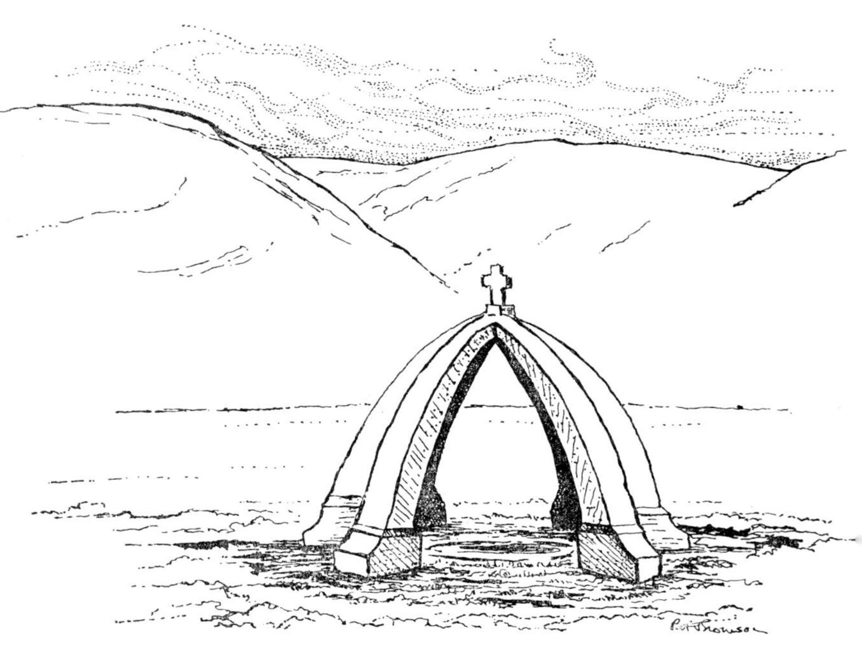

Queen's Well

(Built over a spring by the Earl of Dalhousie to commemorate the place where Queen Victoria and her party stopped to refresh themselves on a visit to Glenesk in 1861)

The Episcopal church, anyway, was not the only one in the Glen that suffered in time of war. So too did the church that is so picturesquely set on the shore of Loch Lee. A century earlier it had to be rebuilt after being destroyed by the Marquis of Montrose. Its graveyard is of special renown, for it was the last resting place of Alexander Ross, poet and schoolmaster at Lochlee. Two of the epitaphs on stones in the graveyard are attributed to Ross's pen. He became a poet of national standing— Robert Burns was one of his admirers — and his songs are still sung and enjoyed today.

In the 17th and early 18th centuries the national quest for bullion and minerals was echoed in the Glen and the workings at the silver mines on Craig Soales and Gilfumman can still be seen. German and Flemish miners were in charge. But there is little evidence of the quantity or the quality of the ore extracted.

By that time the Gaelic language had died out in Glenesk, though it still lingers on in such lovely place names as Monawee, Glas Corrie, Corriehausherin, Murmannoch, Maolern and Badalair, to name only a few.

In the nineteenth century Queen Victoria purchased Balmoral and her annual visits to her Deeside estates brought an economic change to the entire area. The tradition of deer forests, grouse moors and shooting lodges became firmly established and it has come right down to the present time. For many years the Glen boasted of three shooting lodges, Invermark, the Retreat and Millden, each with its own grouse moor. But now the Retreat houses a Folk Museum, tearoom and shop which have become major attractions in the summer months.

Past and Present

IF YOU are accustomed to tight timetables, to work schedules by day and endless commuting each morning and evening, the pattern of life in this lovely glen must seem a leisurely one. But you could be wrong. The land and the love of the land are firm taskmasters.

Admittedly there are no set working hours — only patterns to be adhered to in a working day, be the person farmer or game-keeper. And these, today, are the two main occupations. In time past, when the area was more densely populated, there were soutars, blacksmiths, joiners, millers and other tradesmen. Day labourers too could earn a living by making ditches, peat-cutting, harvesting, wood-cutting and all the other jobs that create rural living. But depopulation and automation have largely brought an end to those local crafts.

Only the weather has changed little. It still plays its vital part in workaday life. Winter blizzards mean sitting tight until they blow over, then buckling to and clearing roads and making good any damage done. Rain during haymaking stops the mowing and turning of the crop. You have to wait until everything has dried out. Sheep shearing may have to be postponed for the same reason — and days on the grouse moor, when thick mist and torrential rain spell utter misery for shooting tenant and ghillie alike. But this means having to catch up on chores when the opportunity comes, to fit them back into the pattern of the year.

Though bonus schemes, overtime and double time may be vastly important elsewhere, here the people just work on until the task is done. When the weather is settled for hay-making, the sound of the mower can be heard far into the summer evenings until the dew comes down and work perforce must stop. And when fox-hunting begins the gamekeepers' day starts

Cutting the Hay Crop

before the dawning. After hours on the hill they come down to perform their daily chores and often they round off the day on the hill again, checking the dens at nightfall.

In many ways the pattern and economics of Glen life have changed since World War II. Long before then the Glen was already popular with summer visitors. "Lang Tam" Guthrie, the great Edinburgh philanthropist who founded schools for the poor last century, was one who came regularly as a visitor. But still the Glen remained in large part an enclosed and self-sufficient community. In a very real sense, most householders lived off the land. Meal, potatoes, turnips and other such staples were stored in girnels, kists and outside pits, and most people kept a pig, to be slaughtered and salted down at the back end of the year. Most households too had a cow which gave them milk, butter and cheese in plenty for the greater part of the year. They organised things so that the cow went into calf when the extra milk was needed — maybe to feed orphan lambs during the lambing season or to meet extra demands by summer visitors.

The time for peat-cutting was in between the sowing and the thinning of the turnip crop. And the turnips, by tradition, were lifted and pitted before the Masonic Ball in November.

Time has changed those customs. Now that animal foodstuffs cost so much, far fewer people keep hens, ducks and pigs. The turnip crop is generally left in the fields and the animals are turned in to feed, a section at a time. Marauding deer love this new method. They despoil whole fields of neeps with their random bites in the night-time.

The rabbit, unknown north of the Tay until the nineteenth century, was something of a novelty when it was first introduced. You can read how the rabbit "supporters" of yesteryear even advocated the construction of warrens, lovingly dug by man himself, to give the bunny every chance to be fruitful and multiply. And trouble could be in store for anyone who took a rabbit without permission. It was some time before their nuisance value was really appreciated.

The rabbit population explosion had quite a serious effect on hill farming. It meant not only a loss of precious pasture but the ground was fouled as well, and farmers discovered that sheep

Grouse Beating

would not graze where rabbit infestation was high. It caused a drop in fleece quality too. So the farmer turned to the rabbit as a source of supplementing his income. There are still people in the glen who can recall when the sale of rabbit carcases helped to pay farm rents. Right up to the advent of myxomatosis, the rabbit lorry was a regular sight on the glen road.

Now even the milk cows have dwindled in numbers. The majority of "glenners", like city dwellers, have their milk supplied by dairies.

Sheep-shearing, however, is one custom which still adheres to tradition. Even the modern electric shears have not entirely ousted the hand shears. And clippings, like other jobs which require additional labour, are still carried out under the old system known as Love-darging, where services are returned for services rendered. Those clippings are highly sociable affairs with an air of lighthearted fun though the work goes on unceasingly.

In the pre-car, pre-television era, rural communities had to create their own amusements and often the folk would gather in some neighbour's house for an evening's music, cards or story-telling. A really good fiddle player was a pearl beyond price and many an evening the rafters dirled with the lilt of strathspeys, jigs and reels, interspersed with pawky humour. Dancing is still a popular pastime but many of the old traditional favourites — like the Polka Mazurka, Waltz Cotillion and La Vas — live on only in the memories of the older generation.

Many people speak of depopulation as if it was a problem of the past and not of the present. But though the trend started a long time ago, it still continues. Small acreages become unviable and there is always the problem that the glen offers school leavers nothing by way of jobs. So the Glen becomes emptier with every passing decade. No one can foresee where it will end but future generations are going to be the poorer if local folk and their couthiness must vanish entirely from the scene.

SOUPS

Tormentil

Hay-fit, stray-fit,
Hay-fit,
NOO!

This ditty was used by bothy-lads in the teaching of pas-de-bas, a basic step in Scottish country dancing. A straw was inserted in the left boot and a piece of hay in the right.

CLEAR BORTSCH SOUP

1 quart of good clear stock made from beef and some duck bones if possible.
2 medium raw beetroot.
1 large onion.
Stick of celery or celery salt.
Bay leaf, thyme and parsley.
1 teaspoon tarragon vinegar.
A few drops of lemon juice or malt vinegar.
Seasoning.

Peel and slice raw beetroot and place in dish with a peeled and sliced raw onion, bay leaf, a good sprig of parsley and thyme.

Sprinkle with the tarragon vinegar and a few drops of lemon juice or malt vinegar.

Cover with plate and leave at least one hour.

Empty contents into top of double saucepan, or a saucepan or casserole which can stand in a tin of water in the oven.

Add stock and seasoning, and heat slowly for at least one hour. Make very hot but do *not* let it boil.

Have ready a Julienne of cooked beetroot, put into a tureen and make hot. Taste soup for seasoning — it should be sharp, but not too acid. Strain carefully into tureen. It should be bright red and clear.

Whip cream and add a teaspoon of lemon juice. Serve as an accompaniment to the soup.

Mrs Cruickshank,
Invermark Lodge.

THICK BORTSCH SOUP

$\frac{1}{4}$ lb raw shin of beef, knuckle bone, or pieces of duck if possible.
Large raw beetroot, onion, leek, carrot, celery, tomato, bay leaf, parsley, thyme, seasoning.
Lemon juice, tarragon vinegar.
Butter or bacon fat, cornflour.
Sour cream or whipped cream with squeeze of lemon juice to be served separately.

Cut up beef in small pieces. Put knob of butter or bacon fat in thick saucepan and heat. Add beef and cook till slightly brown. Add knuckle bone plus any other pieces and a quart of water. Season and bring slowly to the boil. Skim any scum from the surface. Add all peeled sliced vegetables and herbs. Bring to boil again and simmer for about an hour. Mix sufficient cornflour to thicken soup slightly, allow to boil for a few more minutes, then remove meat and bones and put the remainder through moulin strainer. Return to pan and add shredded pieces of meat. Add lemon juice and tarragon vinegar, then reheat and serve.

Mrs Cruickshank,
Invermark Lodge.

A Nineteenth Century Kitchen Interior

GAME BROTH

The remains of game.
1 quart of stock or water.
3 - 4 ozs ham or bacon.
2 ozs flour
1 onion.
1 carrot.
2 sticks celery.
1 bunch herbs.
Salt and pepper.

Shred the vegetables finely.

Heat a little fat in the pan, add the game, herbs, ham and seasoning, and simmer for two hours.

Heat 2 ozs fat in a pan, add flour and brown thoroughly.

Strain the stock on to the flour, stirring carefully; add the finely shredded vegetables and some pieces of game and cook for a further 20 minutes before serving.

Mrs R. Forbes,
Woodhaugh.

HARE SOUP

Reserve some of the blood.

Boil the basket (rib cage) and the bones for 2 hours.

Stew back and hind legs with a little seasoning until tender, then either mince or pound the meat.

Strain stock and add meat, carrots and onions, adjust seasoning, and simmer gently until the chopped or shredded vegetables are thoroughly cooked.

Mix the blood with cornflour to a paste and add to the soup. When serving, pour a dash of port wine in bottom of tureen and pour soup over.

Miss M. Stewart,
Buskhead.

LEEK AND POTATO SOUP

3 large leeks.
2 pints stock (mutton stock is excellent for this).
1½ *lbs potatoes.*
½ *gill milk.*
½ *gill cream.*
1½ *ozs butter or margarine.*
1 carrot.
Seasoning.
Chopped parsley.

Chop the leeks roughly, using some of the green for colour.

Melt the butter in the pan and cook the leeks gently in this for 5 - 10 minutes, taking care that they do not brown.

Add the sliced potatoes, carrots, seasoning and stock and bring to the boil.

Simmer for 1½ hours, then sieve and return to pan.

Add milk and cream and reheat but do *not* boil.

Mrs J. Carnegie,
Invermark.

FISH

Primrose

Tadpole Collectors

NORMANDY HADDOCK
(Serves four or five)

6 medium filleted haddock.
½ oz. butter.
2 tablespoons white wine.
Pepper and salt.
1 teaspoonful dried thyme.
½ teacup chopped parsley.
1 medium sized onion or shallot.
⅓ pint cream.

Grease a casserole thickly with butter.

Cut the fish into pieces about three inches long and lay on bottom of casserole. Season with salt and pepper and sprinkle with parsley and thyme. Add finely chopped onion or shallot.

Pour wine over and leave for about one hour to marinate.

Pour the cream over the top and bake in a moderate oven — 350° to 375° for 20 minutes.

A little parmesan cheese can be sprinkled over the top, if desired, 5 minutes before serving.

Mrs J. Carnegie,
Invermark.

SPAGHETTI AND FISH PIE (Hot)

1 tin spaghetti in tomato sauce.
Skin and bone pieces of any type of white fish.
A little grated onion.
Flour.
Pepper and salt.
Chopped parsley (fresh or dried).
Squeeze of lemon juice.
Mashed potato.
A little grated cheese.
Knob of butter or margarine.

Grease a shallow pie dish with butter and put spaghetti in bottom.

Roll the pieces of fish well in flour, season, and lay on top of spaghetti.

Sprinkle with onion, chopped parsley and a good squeeze of lemon juice.

Cook and mash potatoes with margarine and pepper, adding milk to ensure that mixture is fairly soft.

Spread over top of fish and seal dish right over with potatoes.

Sprinkle over grated cheese and dot with margarine.

Stand dish in tin containing a little water and bake at 350° for about an hour or until top of pie is a light golden brown.

Mrs Cruickshank,
Invermark Lodge.

SALMON AND MACARONI PIE

2 ozs cooked macaroni.
½ pint milk.
Seasoning.
1 lb cooked salmon.
½ oz flour.
Juice of half a lemon.

Place macaroni in pan, cover with nearly all the milk and bring to boiling point.

Blend flour with rest of milk and add to macaroni, stirring till it thickens.

Add salmon and seasoning.

Place in greased dish and place breadcrumbs and dots of butter on top.

Bake in hot oven until nicely browned.

The late Mrs Caithness,
Heatherbank.

SMOKED HADDOCK PATE (Cold)

1 large smoked haddock.
¼ lb butter (or butter and margarine mixed).
Pepper.
2 teaspoonfuls lemon juice.
2 tablespoons whipped cream.
A little extra butter.

Place haddock in greased dish, covered in buttered paper, and cook in moderate oven for long enough to separate skin and bone from the flesh. Either mince the fish or put through liquidiser.

Melt butter gently but do not make hot.

Add pepper and lemon juice to fish and gradually mix in melted butter. When well mixed, stir in a quantity of whipped cream, the amount depending on the size of fish.

Taste for seasoning.

Place mixture in dish and cover with more melted butter and place in refrigerator to firm.

Serve either as a first course with hot toast or with biscuits for a snack.

Mrs Cruickshank,
Invermark Lodge.

GAME

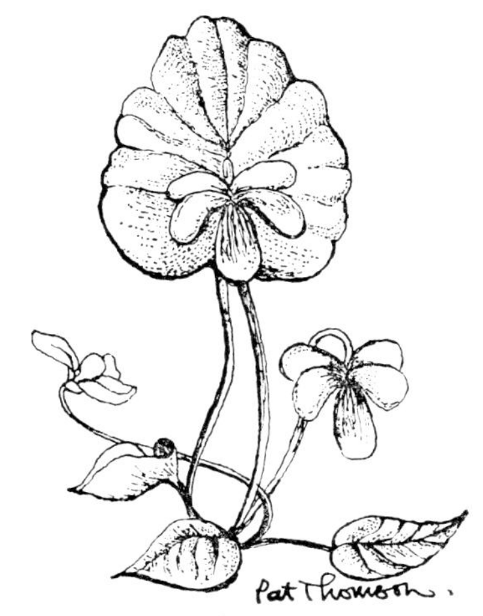

Violet

RABBIT PIE

1 rabbit.
¼ lb bacon.
½ teaspoon salt.
¼ teaspoon pepper.
1 hard-boiled egg.
1 teaspoon chopped parsley.
Pinch chopped herbs.
Grated lemon rind.
½ gill stock.
Rough puff pastry made with 5 ozs flour and 3¾ ozs margarine.

Chop parsley and mix all seasonings. Wash, dry and joint rabbit and dip in seasonings. Place a layer in bottom of pie dish, then a layer of bacon, cut in slices, and lastly a hard-boiled egg, sliced. Continue to fill dish with these layers. Add stock, cover with pastry and bake in a very hot oven for the first ten minutes, then lower heat and cook for 1½ - 2 hours.

The late Mrs Caithness,
Heatherbank.

RABBIT ROLL

Take 1 lb minced rabbit and ½ lb minced bacon, and mix with ½ lb breadcrumbs, ¼ pint milk, 1 teaspoon salt, pepper and 2 eggs. Place in jar and steam for two hours.

Mrs H. Ferrier,
Cuttlehaugh.

RABBIT PUDDING

1 rabbit.
1 onion.
1 teaspoon sage.
2 large potatoes.
8 ozs flour.
2 ozs fat.
2 ozs grated raw potato.
1 teaspoon baking powder.
Salt and pepper.

Mix flour, baking powder, a pinch of salt, grated potato and fat, then make into a dry dough with very little water. Roll out thinly and use two-thirds to line a pudding basin.

Joint rabbit and put into pudding along with diced potatoes, onion and seasoning. Add a little water and cover with remaining dough. Cover with greased paper and steam for two hours.

The late Mrs Caithness,
Heatherbank.

STUFFED RABBIT

1 rabbit.
4 ozs oatmeal (approximately).
2 ozs suet.
1 onion.

Thoroughly wash and clean rabbit.

Mix oatmeal, suet and chopped onion, and stuff rabbit with this mixture and sew up. Stew or roast until rabbit is tender.

Mrs H. Dickson,
Druid's Knowe.

TERRINE OF VENISON (Cold)

5 ozs. meat which has been finely minced, along with one pork sausage and 1 oz streaky bacon.

Mix with one egg yolk and one tablespoonful sherry or red wine. Season with pepper, salt and a little nutmeg.

Line dish with thin rashers of streaky bacon and put in half of mixture and press down.

Place yolk of hard-boiled egg in centre along with a little chopped ham. Cover with rest of mixture, finishing with a layer of streaky bacon.

Put lid on dish and stand in a tin of water. Cook in a moderate oven for approximately 1½ hours.

When cooked, turn upside down and place a weight on top.

Serve cold.

Liver or game can also be used in this dish.

Mrs Cruickshank,
Invermark Lodge.

Going to Church Pre-1920

HAGGIS — FOR A CHANGE

Much has been written and recorded of the "war effort" made by those at home in both the Great Wars — the knitting of socks, balaclavas and comforters being one of the contributions made by womenfolk all over the country.

Mrs Dickson of Dalbrack was, however, a little more original in her contribution to front line troops, as she made quantities of haggis which she packed in earthenware "jeely jars" and had despatched to the battlefields of France and Belgium.

These must have been a welcome change for the homesick "sodger" after an unrelenting diet of "bully beef".

There are veterans of World War I who have not allowed corned beef to pass their lips since Armistice was declared in 1918!

VENISON HAGGIS

Boil liver and heart for two hours.

Grate part of the liver, then mince the rest with the heart and two or three onions and mix with half a pound of suet.

Toast one and a half breakfastcupfuls of oatmeal slowly and add to mixture.

Season and pour over 1 -1½ pints pluck brie to give a fairly soft consistency.

The mixture can then be either steamed in a bowl for two hours or cooked in the pluck (stomach). The latter entails the scraping and cleaning of the bag after boiling and it then has to be sewn, after being filled with the mixture. It must also be pricked frequently whilst cooking. Care must be taken not to overfill the bag — allow plenty of room for the mixture to expand.

Also, to facilitate removal from the pot after cooking, it is advisable to set a tea towel on top of the plate (plate is necessary on bottom of pot to prevent haggis from sticking). It is then simply a matter of grasping the towel and lifting out the haggis without the risk of bursting it.

The above dish, along with chappit neeps, tatties, cloutie dumpling and shortbread, is served at the annual Burns Nicht in January. People come from a' the airts to sample the above fare and, judging by its popularity, venison haggis must surely be the supreme chieftain o' a' the puddens!

POULTRY

Lady's Smock

Feeding the Hens

CHICKEN FERMIERE (Hot)

Joint chicken and put into stew pan along with a knob of butter. Cover, and allow to cook for a few minutes without browning, then turn and cook gently on other side.

Add:

A good cupful of rice.
1 finely sliced onion.
2 sliced carrots.
1 head of celery, sliced.
1 small bay leaf.
Pinch of thyme and parsley.
Pepper and salt.

Add enough chicken stock to make it moist, plus two tablespoons white wine if desired.

Put on lid and cook slowly in oven for about 1½ hours, adding a little more stock from time to time if necessary.

Add a good squeeze of lemon juice if no wine has been used and sprinkle with chopped parsley prior to serving.

The mixture, when ready, should be fairly dry.

Pheasant or pieces of lamb can be cooked equally well in this way.

Mrs Cruickshank,
Invermark Lodge.

CHARTRES PIE (Cold)

Cut some boiled chicken into fairly large pieces and season with pepper, salt, a scraping of onion and a few drops of tarragon vinegar.

Whip half a pint of cream — quantity depends on how much chicken is used.

Add a large teaspoon tomato ketchup to the cream and mix in with chicken. Have ready a cold baked puff pastry case, fill with mixture and chill well before serving.

Decorate with chopped parsley.

Mrs Cruickshank,
Invermark Lodge.

ROMAN PIE (Hot or Cold)

Line a deep flan ring or shallow cake tin with loose bottom, with short-crust pastry.

Dice some cold cooked turkey or chicken, and a little diced ham. Mix this with two eschalots (finely chopped), a little grated parmesan cheese, thick white sauce (quantity according to size of pie required) and two tablespoons cream. Add a little mixed mustard and season to taste.

Place mixture in pastry case, damp sides and cover top with pastry. Make hole in centre and glaze top with a little beaten egg.

Bake at 375° for $\frac{3}{4}$ - 1 hour.

Serve hot or cold.

Mrs Cruickshank,
Invermark Lodge.

MEAT

Chickweed Wintergreen

Washday (1940s)

BEEF HAMBURGERS (Hot)

8 ozs steak mince.
1 small finely chopped onion.
Chopped parsley.
Pinch of dried thyme.
Salt and pepper.
1 teaspoon tomato ketchup.
Yolk of egg.

Mix mince and herbs well together with a fork and bind with tomato ketchup and yolk of egg.

Heat frying pan and put in a little oil and a knob of butter, sufficient to cover bottom of pan.

Divide mince into six balls, flatten slightly and dip in flour.

Fry for about three minutes, turn, and fry on other side for the same amount of time or longer, according to taste.

Serve with mashed potatoes or spaghetti and fried onions.

Mrs Cruickshank,
Invermark Lodge.

PANHACKILTY

(a recipe which has been in the donor's family for many generations)

Cold cooked meat — corned beef or minced beef.
Onions.
Sliced raw potatoes.

Place layers of meat and sliced onion in flat casserole or meat roasting tin. Make a beef stock, depending on quantity of meat and vegetables used, and pour over.

Cover with thinly sliced potatoes and cook on hot oven until potatoes are almost tender, adding more liquid if necessary.

Half an hour before serving, mix 1 lb S.R. flour with ½ lb grated suet and one finely chopped onion. Mix to a stiff dough with water and place round edges and in corners of tin (suet paste must only be half submerged in gravy). Bake until dumpling mix is hot and brown.

Serve hot.

Mrs J. Keats,
Burnfoot.

An ideal dish for a winter's day.

My mammy says that I must go
To fetch my daddy's denner o,
Chappit tatties, beef and steak,
Twa reid herrin and a bawbee cake.
I cam tae the watter and I couldna get across,
So I peyd ten bob for an auld doon horse,
I louped on its back, and its back gaed a crack,
So I sat and played my fiddle till the boatie cam back.

GROUNDNUT STEW
(Based on a West African dish)

1 lb neck of lamb.
1 large onion.
Fresh tomatoes to taste or one small tin tomato puree.
1 large tablespoon peanut butter.
Salt.
Black pepper, freshly ground.
Long grain rice.
Fat or butter.

Dice onions and cook in heated fat without browning, then add diced meat and cook until thoroughly browned. Season with salt and pepper. This is traditionally a hot spicy dish but the quantity of pepper added will depend on individual taste.

Add tomatoes and sufficient meat stock (a beef cube made up according to instructions will suffice) to cover. Add peanut butter, stirring well, and cook gently for two hours.

Serve with a border of boiled rice.

Any other of the cheaper cuts of meat or pork go well in the above recipe.

P. Thomson.

HUNT PIE

2 - 4 ozs lentils.
2 ozs mince.
¾ lb mixed vegetables.
1 Oxo cube.
¾ pint water.
Seasoning.
Pastry.
2 ozs flour.
2 ozs oatmeal.
½ teaspoon baking powder.
Salt.
Water.

Brown mince. Mix cube with water and place with rest of ingredients in a pie dish.

PASTRY.—Mix dry ingredients and bind with water. Roll out, cover mixture, and cook for ½ - ¾ hour in a moderate oven.

Mrs Caithness,
Heatherbank.

JUGGED BEEF

2 - 3 lbs shin of beef.
1 large onion.
6 cloves.
1 teacupful breadcrumbs.
1 glass claret or port.
Pepper and salt.

Cut the shin into pieces and place in a casserole with water. Add the onion with the cloves stuck in it.

Cover, place in oven and stew for 4 hours. Test to see if tender and add seasoning. Add breadcrumbs ten minutes before serving. Lastly, add claret or port.

Serve in a deep dish with a border of macaroni.

The late Mrs Caithness,
Heatherbank.

STEAK IN BLACK BUTTER

Frying steak.
Large knob of butter.

Heat butter in frying pan until smoking hot, then put in steak and sear quickly on both sides to seal in the juices.

Lower heat and cook until some juice appears on top of steak.

Serve on heated plate with butter poured over steak as a sauce.

Creamed potatoes and grilled tomatoes make the best accompaniment to this dish.

P. Thomson.

Speedwell

LUNCHEONS FOR PARTRIDGE SHOOT PICNICS

Stuffed Shrimp Eggs

Goulash of Beef
Brussels Sprouts
Potatoes

Apple Puffs

Cheese, biscuits and celery

Coffee

Lentil Soup

Cold Chicken Pie
Cold Ham
Salad
Baked Potatoes

Cold Omnibus Pudding
with Whipped Cream

Cheese and Biscuits

Coffee

HOT SWEETS

Tormentil

Knock at the door,
Peep in,
Lift the latch,
Wipe your feet,
And wauk in.

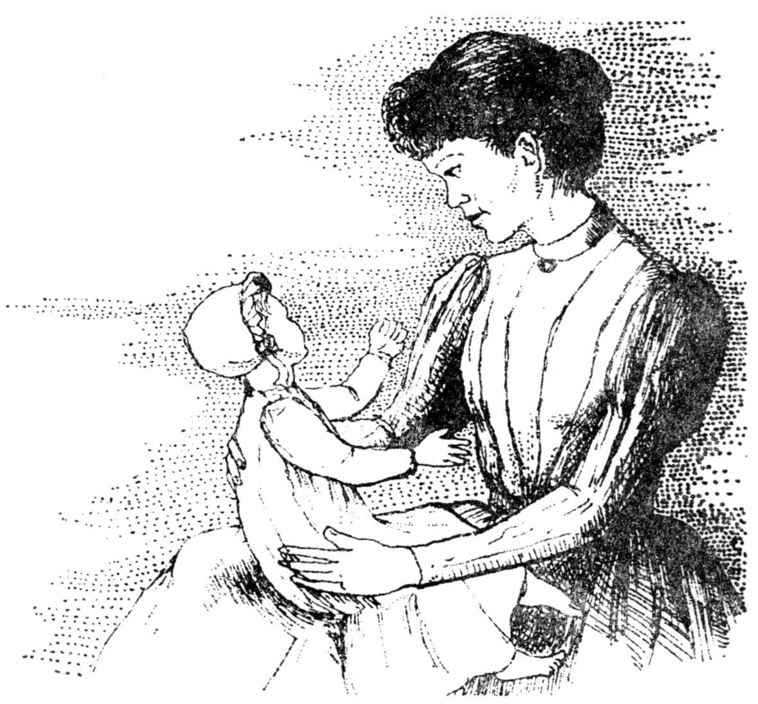

APPLES WITH DUNFILLAN PASTE

4 tablespoons flour.
3 ozs butter.
2 tablespoons sugar.
$\frac{1}{4}$ pint milk.
$1\frac{1}{2}$ lbs apples.
1 egg.
Pinch baking powder.
Flavouring to taste.

Have ready some cold stewed apples.

Rub butter into flour and add baking powder.

Beat up egg with sugar, add milk and stir into flour.

Mix well, pour on top of apples and bake in a moderate oven for 30 minutes.

Any other kind of stewed fruit goes equally well with this paste.

Mrs A. Kirkland,
Tarfside Post Office.

GINGERBREAD PUDDING (Hot)

4 ozs flour.
4 ozs margarine.
4 ozs breadcrumbs.
4 ozs syrup.
4 ozs demerara sugar.
1 teaspoon ground ginger.
½ teaspoon bicarbonate of soda.
Pinch of salt.
Milk to mix.

Sieve flour, ginger and salt into basin and rub in margarine. Add breadcrumbs and sugar and mix well. Put syrup in well in centre.

Warm one teacupful of milk and dissolve soda in it. Add to mixture and blend well together — the mix should be fairly soft. Put into greased basin, cover and steam for 2½ hours.

Turn out and serve with syrup or custard.

Mrs Cruickshank,
Invermark Lodge.

MARMALADE PUDDING (Hot)

5 ozs breadcrumbs.
3 ozs suet.
1 oz demerara sugar.
2 tablespoons marmalade.
1 beaten egg and a little milk.
½ teaspoon bicarbonate of soda.
Extra marmalade for garnish.
Whipped cream.

Mix suet with breadcrumbs and sugar. Place 2 tablespoonfuls of marmalade in centre. Mix soda with the beaten eggs and milk, then mix all well together, adding a little more milk if necessary. Put into greased basin and steam for one and a half hours.

Turn out, and serve with hot marmalade around the pudding and accompany with cream, served separately in a sauce boat.

GUARDS PUDDING

Use strawberry jam and grated rind of lemon in place of marmalade.

Mrs Cruickshank,
Invermark Lodge.

Blackness

CLOUTIE DUMPLING

3 cups flour.
1 cup currants.
2 cups raisins.
1 cup sugar.
1 cup chopped suet.
1 teaspoon baking soda.
1 teaspoon cream of tartar.
1 tablespoon treacle.
1 tablespoon syrup.
1 teaspoon ground ginger.
1 teaspoon cinnamon.
Milk to mix.

Mix dry ingredients.

Add treacle and syrup, melted in a little hot water and enough milk to make a stiff batter.

Scald cloth, which is best made of calico or a material of similar strength; wring out and dredge with flour.

Tie, making sure there is room allowed for expansion, and boil for 3 - 4 hours.

Place plate below dumpling whilst cooking.

The late Mrs R. Davidson,
Blackness.

(A favourite method of serving left-over dumpling is to heat some butter in a frying pan, cook dumpling fairly quickly in this, and serve dredged with caster sugar).

CROFTERS' PLUM PUDDING

½ lb breadcrumbs.
½ lb flour.
8 ozs suet.
8 ozs raisins.
6 ozs brown sugar.
1 teaspoon baking soda.
1 teaspoon cinnamon.
1 teaspoon allspice.
1 - 2 eggs.
Treacle — to taste.
Milk to mix.

Mix dry ingredients.

Warm milk and treacle (enough to melt treacle) and mix in baking soda. Add to dry ingredients along with beaten eggs. This should make a fairly soft dough.

Wring out strong cloth in boiling water and flour well. Put in mixture, tie securely and steam for 2½ - 3 hours.

Alternatively, steam pudding in greased bowl but allow an extra hour in cooking time.

Mrs S. D. Michie,
Cairncross.

GOOSEBERRY DUMPLING
(A very old recipe)

1 lb gooseberries.
4 ozs suet.
4 ozs brown sugar.
½ lb flour.
Pinch of salt.

Top and tail gooseberries and put in a basin with all the other ingredients.

Slowly pour in enough water to form a fairly soft dough.

Boil for two hours in a greased pudding basin or a floured cloth.

Serve with whipped cream and soft brown sugar.

Mrs J. Keats,
Burnfoot.

FREE KIRK PUDDING

(So-called because it contains no egg)

2 tablespoons flour.
2 tablespoons currants.
2 tablespoons raisins.
2 tablespoons breadcrumbs.
2 tablespoons ground rice.
2 tablespoons sugar.
3 tablespoons suet.
½ teaspoon mixed spice.
½ teaspoon baking soda.
1 tablespoon treacle.

Mix dry ingredients and add milk and treacle. Place in bowl and steam for 2 - 3 hours.

Mrs A. Kirkland,
Tarfside Post Office.

SWISS APPLES

Cooking apples.
Pieces of stale bread, brown or white.
Demerara sugar.
Grated rind of 1 lemon or 4 cloves.
Golden syrup.
Butter.
Spoonful of water.

Butter a pie dish.

Dice crusts of bread, make rough crumbs with the rest and cover the bottom of the dish with the crumbs.

Peel and slice apples and place half in dish. Cover apples with breadcrumbs, demerara sugar, half lemon rind and 2 cloves.

Put rest of apples on top and cover with diced crusts, sugar, lemon rind (or remaining 2 cloves), 1 tablespoonful syrup and a tablespoonful of water. Dot with butter and bake at 350° for about one hour or until apples are cooked and brown on top.

Alternatively, gooseberries, plums and rhubarb can be used in this particular sweet.

Mrs Cruickshank,
Invermark Lodge.

PINEAPPLE FLUFF

1 small tin pineapple.
2 ozs cornflour
½ pint milk.
2 eggs.
½ oz sugar.
½ pint pineapple juice.

Boil milk and sugar. Mix the cornflour with the juice and add it to the milk. Boil for two minutes, stirring well.

Remove from the heat and beat in the egg yolks. Add some cut-up pineapple. Pour into a greased pie dish. Whisk the egg whites until quite stiff and spread over the mixture. Sprinkle well with caster sugar. Decorate with some of the pineapple and bake until the egg white is set and slightly browned.

Mrs R. Forbes,
Woodhaugh.

COLD SWEETS

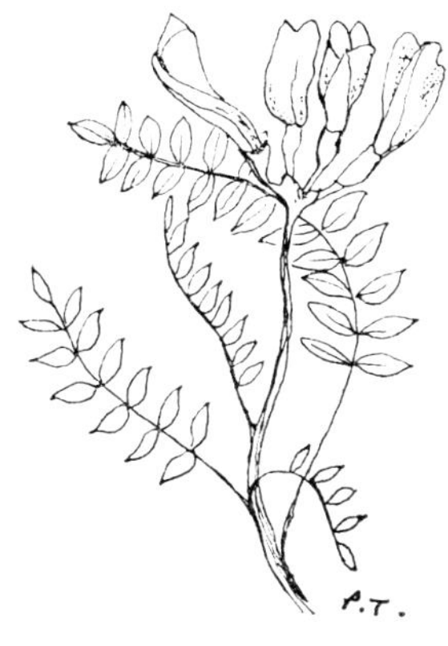

Vetch

Sunday Best (1870s)

CHOCOLATE PROFITEROLES

Put ¼ pint of water in a saucepan with 2 ozs of butter and, when boiling, mix in quickly 2½ ozs sifted flour. Stir until well mixed, then allow to cool slightly. Mix in 2 small eggs, beating well, and add a few drops of vanilla essence.

Place teaspoonfuls on baking sheet and bake in a moderate oven for twenty-five to thirty minutes.

Split holes in sides and allow to cool.

Fill with whipped cream, flavoured with vanilla and caster sugar, and arrange on a shallow glass dish and spoon over a cold chocolate sauce.

Chocolate Sauce

Break up 3 ozs plain chocolate in pan, add one dessertspoon caster sugar and enough water to cover; melt and allow to boil for a few minutes.

Remove from heat, add a knob of butter and vanilla essence, and beat well. Allow to become quite cold before serving.

Mrs Cruickshank,
Invermark Lodge.

CARROT TORTE

Separate four eggs.

Beat whites until stiff and then beat in ¼ cup sugar and set aside.

Beat egg yolks until thick and lemon coloured, then beat in ¾ cup sugar.

Add 1 cup grated raw carrot, grated rind of one lemon, juice of half lemon, ½ cup flour and 1 teaspoon baking powder.

Fold in beaten egg whites.

Bake in two nine-inch cake pans.

When cool, put together with whipped cream.

Mrs J. Keats,
Burnfoot.

CREAM OF APPLES

2 lbs apples.
½ pint milk.
½ pint cream.
½ lemon
2 ozs sugar.
Glace cherries.
Ratafias.

Peel and cut up apples and stew slowly in a little water, along with the grated rind of half lemon. Add sugar to taste.

Boil milk and cream together and add this gradually to stewed apples. When nearly cold, pour mixture into a silver or cut glass dish and decorate with cherries and ratafias.

Mrs J. Keats,
Burnfoot.

FRUIT TORTE

1 packet puff pastry.
1 carton double cream.
Fresh raspberries or strawberries.
Walnuts.
Cooking chocolate.

Break cooking chocolate into small pieces, place in bowl and melt in pan of hot water.

Roll out pastry into oblong shape, place on greased tray and bake at 425°. Make sure it is thoroughly baked before removing from oven, otherwise it may partially collapse instead of being firm and well-risen.

Allow to cool, then split and fill base with fruit.

Whip cream, sweeten with a little sugar, and stir in chopped walnuts, reserving a few for decoration.

Spoon cream on top of fruit and put on pastry lid.

Spread top with melted chocolate and decorate with walnuts.

P. Thomson.

PEPPERMINT SWEET

Make up one packet of gelatine according to instructions on packet. Allow to cool slightly, then add peppermint essence to taste, a little green colouring and sugar.

Whip one carton double cream and fold in when jelly has almost set.

Spoon into individual glasses and allow to set firmly.

Decorate with sprigs of fresh mint prior to serving.

This is a deliciously cool sweet and is also light and refreshing on hot days.

P. Thomson.

SWISS APPLE CHARLOTTE

Cooking apples.
Double cream.
Syrup.
Cornflakes.

Peel, slice and cook apples with a little water and sugar to taste, then allow to become quite cold.

Whip cream, fold into apple mixture and place in glass dish.

Heat syrup sufficiently to become slightly runny and mix with cornflakes.

Cool, then spoon mixture over apples and cream, and chill in refrigerator before serving.

If desired, a squeeze of lemon juice can be added to the cooked apples to give a sharper taste to this sweet.

P. Thomson.

"Yoursel an' me
Went out to tea
With Sally Magee
And she spilt her tea
All over me . . . "

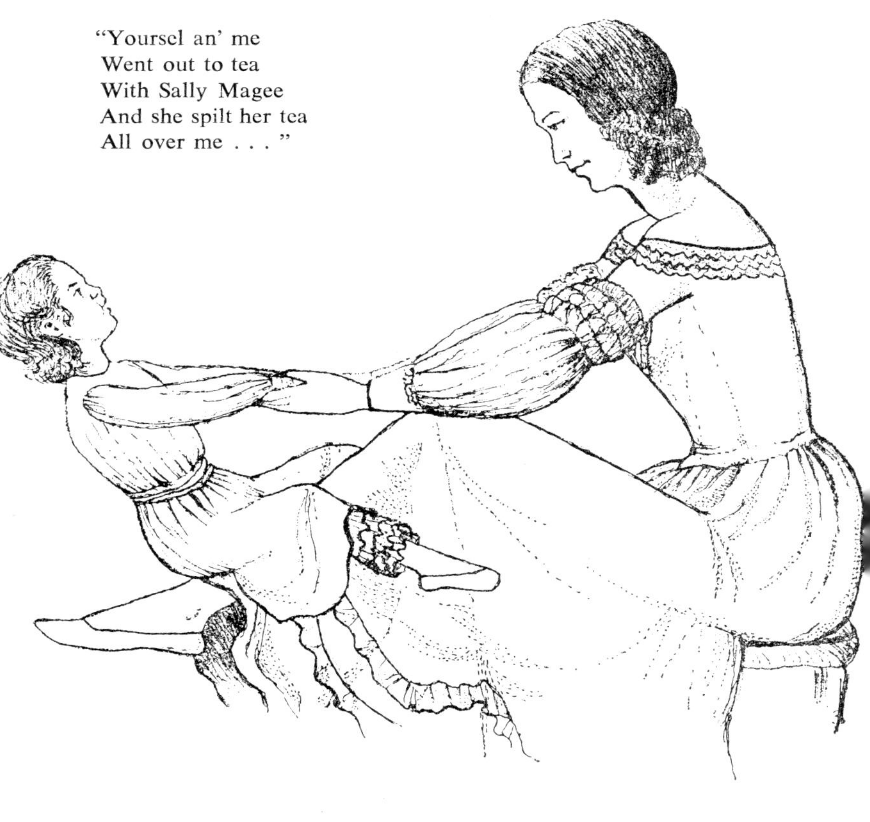

P.T.
Marsh Marigold.

ROULAGE AU CHOCOLAT

5 eggs.
6 ozs caster sugar.
6 ozs plain chocolate.
½ pint cream (whipped).

Cut up chocolate in small pieces and melt in ½ gill water.

Line heavy baking tray with greaseproof paper. Grease thoroughly and set oven at 350°.

Cream egg yolks and sugar till light and white. Stir in cold chocolate melted to a cream with water. Fold in egg whites, stiffly whisked.

Spread on baking tray and bake for about twelve minutes.

Wring out cloth in cold water and lay over tray.

Leave overnight.

Turn out on icing-sugared paper.

Spread with cream.

Roll out (broad side) and dust with icing sugar.

Mrs J. Carnegie,
Invermark.

PINEAPPLE MALLOW

One tin crushed pineapple.
One packet marshmallows.
Double cream

Place pineapple in dish, add chopped marshmallows and mix in thoroughly. (Marshmallows are most easily cut with a pair of scissors. Run water over scissors from time to time to prevent the marshmallows from sticking).

Place mixture in refrigerator and leave overnight.

Whip cream and blend into mixture, then freeze until firm.

P. Thomson.

PETIT GATEAU MONT-ROSE

Take some large castle pudding tins, oil well, and dust with equal quantities of caster sugar and flour.

Make a sponge consisting of

4 ozs margarine
4 ozs caster sugar
2 eggs.
4 ozs self-raising flour.
Grated rind of half a lemon or orange.

Three parts fill tins and bake at 375°. Turn out when cold, carefully slice off top, and scoop out as much of the insides of sponges as possible with a teaspoon.

Whip cream, flavour with caster sugar and vanilla, and fill centres. Put top back on and place upside down on serving dish.

Rub some raspberries through sieve with sufficient caster and icing sugar to sweeten. The puree should be thick. Place in fridge and chill, then spoon over sponge cakes.

(Any fruit in season can be used, and ice cream as an alternative to whipped cream).

Mrs Cruickshank,
Invermark Lodge.

BREAD and SCONES

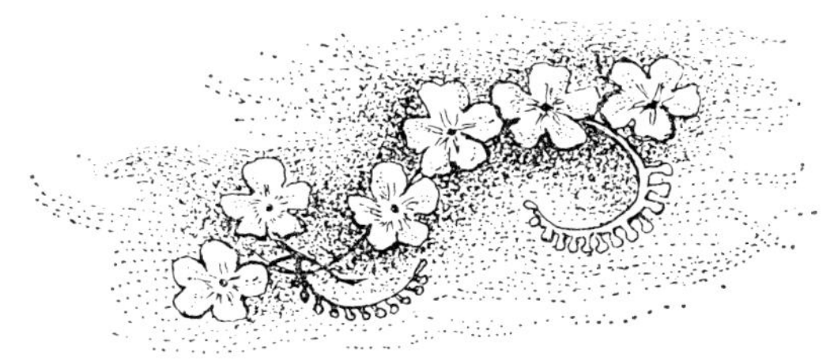

Forget-me-not

Dog Rose

GINGERBREAD (1)

½ lb flour.
4 ozs margarine or lard.
½ teaspoon baking soda.
1 teacup treacle.
1 teacup hot water.
1 teaspoon ground ginger.
3 ozs sugar.
1 egg.
Sultanas.
1 teaspoon cinnamon.

Mix treacle with water, add egg and mix with dry ingredients. Bake in a slow oven for an hour or more.

Mrs R. Osler,
Kirkton, Lochlee.

GINGERBREAD (2)

8 ozs plain flour.
4 ozs soft brown sugar.
4 ozs butter.
1 teaspoon ground ginger.
½ teaspoon baking soda.
8 ozs treacle.
1 gill milk.

Mix dry ingredients.
Warm milk and butter, beat in two eggs and add treacle.
Stir into dry ingredients, beating well.
This mix should be of a runny consistency.
Place in a lined and greased tin and bake for one hour at 300°.

The late Mrs R. Davidson,
Blackness.

RAISIN BREAD

4 teacupfuls self-raising flour.
2 eggs.
½ - ¾ cupful caster sugar.
1 cupful raisins.
Pinch of salt.
3 teaspoonfuls baking powder.
2 teacupfuls milk.

Mix dry ingredients and add fruit, eggs and milk.

The mixture should be a fairly soft one without, however, being a pouring one.

Beat well and place in greased tins which should be three-quarters full.

Tap tins on the table a few times so that the mixture settles smoothly.

Bake for half an hour, starting at 375°, and reducing heat after twenty minutes.

Miss E. Davidson,
Migvie.

SPICE BREAD

Sieve together 12 ozs flour (plain), pinch of salt, 2 level teaspoons baking powder, 1 heaped teaspoon mixed spice.

Rub in 4 ozs margarine.

Stir in ½ lb currants and sultanas.

Warm 4 heaped tablespoons syrup.

Blend in 1 level teaspoon baking soda with one pint milk.

Add, with syrup, to dry ingredients, mixing well.

Bake in lined tin on middle shelf of oven at 325° - 350° for 1½ hours.

Miss E. Caithness,
Heatherbank.

"Ca'in' a Gird"

GIRDLE SCONES

12 ozs plain flour.
1 level teaspoon bicarbonate of soda.
1 heaped teaspoon cream of tartar.
Pinch of salt.
1 dessertspoon caster sugar.
1 oz butter or margarine.
1 egg.
Milk to mix.

The above quantities make about sixteen scones.

Pre-heat girdle. (To test when ready, sprinkle a little dry flour over it — the flour should turn a light golden brown).

Cream butter and sugar till light and fluffy. Add egg and beat thoroughly.

Sieve dry ingredients together and add to creamed mixture alternately with milk, a little at a time, beating thoroughly each time. The mixture should be firm but not too thick.

Have ready a bowl of dry flour. Dip a dessert spoon in milk and then into dry flour and shake off surplus flour.

Take a spoonful of the mixture and drop gently into the flour. (The mixture should just retain the shape of the spoon). Lift gently and toss lightly from hand to hand to remove surplus flour. Lay scone on hot girdle and pat lightly into shape. Cook until golden brown and then turn and cook on other side.

Cool on clean dry towel on wire rack.

Mrs J. Carnegie,
Invermark.

This method of making girdle scones, commonly used in Glenesk, is not widely known in other parts of the country, where the usual practice is to roll the floured dough on a board and cut to shape.

Some housewives prefer to omit the egg, thus giving a whiter scone. Some omit the butter and add a little cream to the batter.

The same mixture can be used to make dropped scones or Scots pancakes in which case a little more milk is added, the girdle greased lightly, and the mixture dropped directly on to the hot girdle in small rounds and turned when brown.

SINGING HINNIES

(A North of England girdle scone)

1 lb plain flour.
4 ozs lard.
4 ozs butter.
¼ teaspoonful salt.
½ teaspoonful cream of tartar.
¼ teaspoonful baking soda.
6 ozs currants.
Sufficient milk to make a stiff dough.

Rub flour, butter and lard together.
Mix in salt, cream of tartar and baking soda.
Add cleaned currants and mix into a firm dough with milk.
Roll out to ¼ in. thickness and cut out with a round cutter.
Bake on a greased hot girdle until one side is brown, then turn, and cook other side.
Split while hot, butter and serve.

Mrs J. Keats,
Burnfoot.

TREACLE SCONES

½ lb plain flour.
A nut of margarine or butter.
2 tablespoons sugar.
2 tablespoons treacle.
½ teaspoon salt.
1 teaspoon baking soda.

Rub margarine into flour and add soda and treacle, salt and sugar. If dough is not quite soft enough, add a little milk.

Roll out, cut, and bake in a moderate oven for 15 - 20 minutes.

Miss D. Skene,
Waterside.

PANCAKES

2½ cups flour.
1 teacup sugar.
2 teaspoons cream of tartar.
1 teaspoon baking soda.
1 cup milk.
2 eggs.
1 tablespoon melted butter.

Mix eggs, butter and milk.
Pour into mixed dry ingredients and blend thoroughly.
Bake on a hot girdle, greasing lightly between each batch.

Miss Michie,
The Retreat.

BISCUITS

Blaeberry

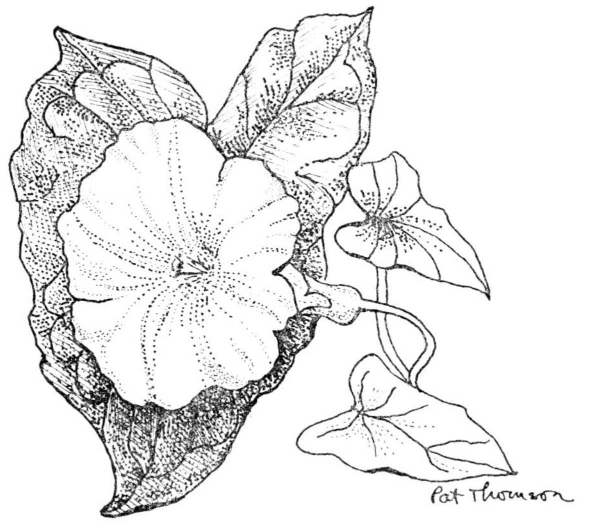

Bindweed

SHORTBREAD (1)

10 ozs plain flour.
4 ozs cornflour.
4 ozs butter.
4 ozs margarine.
1 oz Trex.
4 ozs caster sugar.

Mix all ingredients and knead on board until smooth.
Roll out ¼ in. thick and cut into fingers or rounds and prick.
Bake at 325° - 350° till golden brown. Remove from oven and sprinkle with caster sugar.

Mrs H. Dickson,
Druid's Knowe.

SHORTBREAD (2)

½ lb butter.
¼ lb margarine.
1 teacup caster sugar.
1 handful S.R. flour.
1 handful rice flour (Farola is equally good).
1 lb plain flour (approximately).

Cream butter, margarine and sugar.
Work in rice flour and S.R. flour, then knead until stiff with plain flour.
Roll out, place on greased tins, and mark and prick.
Bake at 325° for about an hour.

Miss M. F. Michie,
The Retreat.

CHEESE BISCUITS

6 ozs flour.
4 ozs cheese.
3 ozs butter.
Salt and cayenne pepper.
1 egg.

Rub butter into flour and grated cheese. Add salt and pepper, and mix to a paste with beaten egg. Roll out and cut into shapes.

Bake in a moderate oven.

Miss E. Campbell,
Kirkton, Lochlee.

CURRANT HEARTS

½ lb flour.
5 ozs butter.
4 ozs currants.
¼ teaspoon baking powder.
1 well-beaten egg.

Rub butter into flour and sugar.
Add currants, baking powder and the egg.
Turn out on to a floured board and roll out one inch thick.
Cut out with a fancy cutter.
Bake in a moderate oven until golden brown.

Miss E. Campbell,
Kirkton, Lochlee.

GINGER BISCUITS

6 ozs flour (S.R.)
¼ teaspoon baking soda.
Pinch salt.
1 teaspoon ground ginger.
3 ozs caster sugar.
4 ozs margarine.
1 tablespoon syrup.

Melt margarine and syrup.
Add to dry ingredients and stir.
Place teaspoonfuls on an ungreased baking sheet.
Bake at 275° for twelve minutes.

Miss P. Davidson,
Blackness.

OAT BISCUITS

2 cupfuls porage oats.
1 cup flour (plain).
1 small cup sugar.
½ lb margarine.

Cream butter and sugar, then gradually mix in flour and oats. Roll out on floured board and cut out.
Bake at 250°.

Mrs G. Strachan,
Milton.

PERKINS

$1\frac{1}{2}$ *cups flour.*
$1\frac{1}{2}$ *cups oatmeal.*
1 cup sugar.
1 beaten egg.
$\frac{1}{4}$ *teaspoon cinnamon.*
$\frac{1}{4}$ *teaspoon ground ginger.*
$\frac{1}{4}$ *teaspoon mixed spice.*
1 teaspoon baking soda.
1 tablespoon syrup.
4 ozs lard.

Mix dry ingredients.
Rub in lard and add egg.
Roll into balls and bake in a moderate oven.

Mrs R. Osler,
Kirkton, Lochlee.

Mallow

GIPSY CREAMS

Take 2 ozs margarine, 2 ozs lard, ½ teacup sugar, 2 teaspoons water and 1 teaspoon syrup. Mix these ingredients in a pan over gentle heat and, when melted, add 1 level teaspoon baking powder, 1 level teaspoon baking soda and 1 level teaspoon vanilla essence.

Stir in one cupful porage oats, 4 ozs plain flour, then make into small balls, place on greased tray and flatten with fork.

Bake for 15 minutes at 350°.

Mrs Osler,
Kirkton, Lochlee.

SABLETS

4 ozs butter.
1 egg.
4 ozs sugar.
2 ozs potato flour (or cornflour).
2 ozs flour.
Chopped almonds.
Grated rind of lemon.

Sieve flours, rub in butter, add lemon rind, sugar and egg.
Roll out to a ¼-in. thickness and cut into fancy shapes.
Sprinkle with chopped almonds.
Bake in a hot oven for about twenty minutes until light golden.

Mrs J. Keats,
Burnfoot.

CAKES and PASTRY

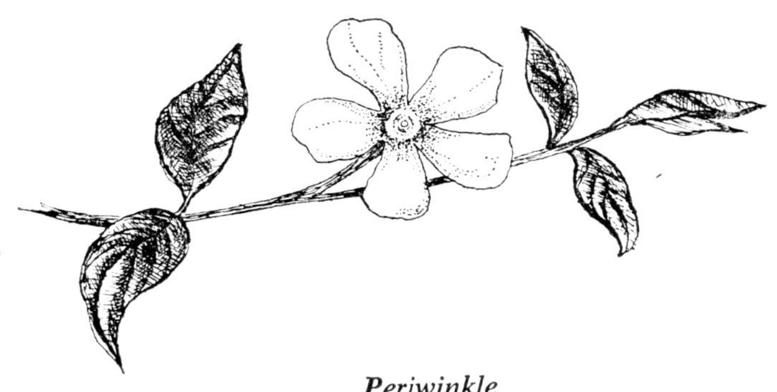

Periwinkle

Rock plants on a dyke

CARAMEL TART

2 ozs margarine.
6 ozs sugar.
2 eggs.
2 cups raisins.
2 teaspoonfuls vanilla essence.
Shortcrust pastry.

Line tin with pastry.
Cream margarine and sugar, add eggs and beat until thick and creamy.
Mix in raisins and essence.
Bake at 350° for 30 minutes.

P. Thomson.

HEDGEHOG CAKE

½ lb butter.
½ lb sugar.
2 tablespoons cocoa.
3 eggs.
1 lb rich tea biscuits.
Vanilla essence to taste.

Mix butter, sugar and cocoa in a saucepan and melt.
When melted, add three beaten eggs and cook until thick.
Remove from heat and mix in flavouring and broken biscuits.
When well mixed, pour into buttered tin and leave for twenty-four hours.
Remove from tin and cut into slices.

Miss E. Caithness,
Heatherbank.

CHRISTMAS CAKE

¾ lb flour.
½ lb butter.
½ lb sugar.
6 ozs currants.
6 ozs sultanas.
1 oz cherries.
6 ozs mixed peel.
1 lemon.
4 eggs.
1 teaspoon mixed spice.
½ teaspoon salt.
4 tablespoons brandy.
½ pint milk.
2 teaspoons baking powder.

Beat butter and sugar to a cream.

Beat eggs and stir in gradually.

Sieve flour, and mix in with salt and spice.

Mix fruit, cherries, lemon peel and mixed peel, and stir into other ingredients.

Add milk and brandy.

Bake in lined tin for 2½ hours, starting at 350° for half an hour, then lowering heat.

The late Mrs Caithness,
Heatherbank.

GINGER TORTE

6 ozs flour.
4 ozs butter.
2 ozs sugar.
2 digestive biscuits.
1 level teaspoon ground ginger.

Cream butter and sugar. Sieve flour and ginger.

Crumble biscuits into butter mixture and blend together all ingredients.

Knead, and place in two tins.

Bake in a moderate oven for 20 minutes.

Turn out and cool.

ICING.—Cream 2 ozs butter with 2 ozs icing sugar and a pinch of ginger, and sandwich together the two halves of the torte.

Miss D. Skene,
Waterside.

RICH PASTRY

8 ozs flour.
5½ *ozs margarine.*
2½ *ozs sugar.*
1 egg.

Cream margarine and sugar.

Add flour and egg alternately, then turn out on to floured board and roll out to required shape.

This is an excellent pastry for fruit pies and tarts.

P. Thomson.

ROCK CAKES

½ lb plain flour.
2 level teaspoons baking powder.
¼ lb margarine.
2 tablespoons granulated sugar.
3 tablespoons demerara sugar.
6 ozs currants.
2 ozs peel.
1 egg.

Rub margarine into dry ingredients.
Mix in egg thoroughly. If mix is too stiff, add a little hot water.
Place spoonfuls on a tray and bake at 350°.

Mrs G. Strachan,
Milton.

(The above must surely be one of the best Rock Cake recipes).

WHISKY CAKE

7 ozs seedless raisins.
¾ pint water.
4 ozs cooking fat.
5 ozs caster sugar.
4 ozs chopped walnuts.
2 or 3 tablespoons whisky.
1 egg.
6 ozs plain flour.
1 level teaspoon baking soda.
¾ teaspoonful ground cloves.
¾ teaspoonful nutmeg.
1 pinch allspice.
1 teaspoonful salt.

Grease and paper two nine-inch sandwich tins.

Cover raisins and simmer for two minutes. Drain, leaving three-quarters of the liquid. Cool. Cream fat and sugar till fluffy and beat in egg. Sift dry ingredients and fold into mixture alternately with liquid. Stir in raisins, nuts and whisky.

Bake at 350° for 30 minutes.

Cool, and sandwich together with some of the filling. Spread rest on top and sides.

FILLING

1 lb icing sugar.
1 small egg.
2 tablespoons whisky.
2 ozs butter.

Cream butter and gradually beat in icing sugar, alternately with lightly beaten egg and whisky.

Mrs J. Carnegie,
Invermark.

SCOTCH CURRANT BUN

Take 1½ breakfastcupfuls of flour and rub in ¼ lb butter or dripping and 1 teaspoonful baking powder. Roll out into a thin sheet.

Grease inside of cake tin and line neatly with paste, reserving a piece for the top of the bun.

Put together in a large basin 1 lb flour, ½ lb sugar, 2 lbs raisins, 2 lbs currants, ¼ lb orange peel, ¼ lb ground almonds, ½ teaspoonful black pepper, ½ oz ginger, ½ oz cinnamon, ½ oz Jamaica pepper, 1 small teaspoon baking soda, 1 teaspoon cream of tartar, 1 breakfastcupful milk, sufficient to moisten.

Mix thoroughly, place in lined tin and flatten top.

Wet edges, seal with pastry lid and prick over with fork.

Bake in a moderate to slow oven.

The late Miss G. Stormonth,
The Haugh.

MISCELLANEOUS

Daisy

Tam, Tam, ye dirty man!
Ye washed yer feet in the fryin' pan.

CAKE IN THE PAN

(This was a one-time favourite at Turnabrane as an afternoon piece or "midser")

Add some currants to a pancake batter and fry in pan with plenty of fat or butter. Turn and serve hot.

This type of dish has the advantage that, while filling, it is easily prepared at a time when "hairsting" and the like make many additional demands on a housewife's time.

CLAPSHOT

Potatoes.
Chives.
Turnips.
Dripping.

Mash together equal quantities of boiled potatoes and turnip.

Add chopped chives, a good piece of dripping, salt and pepper to taste.

Mix thoroughly and serve very hot.

CURRIED EGGS AND BEANS

1 tin baked beans.
Hard-boiled eggs.
Onions.
Curry powder.

Heat a little fat in a pan, add chopped onions and cook lightly but do not allow to brown.

Stir in curry powder according to taste. Blend well, then add beans and eggs.

Cook gently until thoroughly heated.

This is an excellent picnic dish, prepared beforehand, then re-heated over a picnic fire.

P. Thomson.

CRISP ONIONS

Peel and slice a large onion and separate all the rings.

Meanwhile, heat fat or cooking oil in deep pan.

Dip individual rings in milk, then toss in plain flour.

Deep fry until crisp and golden, drain and place in heated dish.

The above make a good accompaniment for steak or hamburgers.

P. Thomson.

FRENCH CHEESE CROUTES

(A teatime snack)

2 slices sandwich pan with the crusts removed.

Spread each slice with a little mustard or chutney.

On one slice place a thin layer of cheese, then a slice of ham and another layer of cheese. Sandwich down with the other slice of bread and press. Cut into four.

Have some cream or top of milk on a plate, dip sandwiches in quickly on both sides and fry until golden brown and warmed through.

Serve hot.

Mrs Cruickshank,
Invermark Lodge.

HAM SAVOURY

1 small chopped onion.
6 ozs chopped ham.
2 egg yolks.
1 tablespoon cream.
½ teaspoon chopped parsley.
Salt and cayenne pepper.
Baked pastry cases.

Fry onion in fat until lightly browned, add ham and stir over low heat until warm.

Beat yolks with cream and blend into ham mixture.

Cook gently until thick.

Stir in chopped parsley and seasoning.

Pile into heated pastry cases and serve hot.

Miss P. Davidson,
Blackness.

MACARONI ANNETTE (Hot)

1 breakfastcup macaroni (cooked).
½ gill water in which macaroni has been cooked.
2 sliced hard-boiled eggs.
4 medium mushrooms, sliced and fried.
1 tablespoon cream.
Pepper and salt.
Butter or margarine.
Cheese souffle sauce.

Butter au gratin dish and put in cooked macaroni, sliced eggs, mushrooms, pepper and salt, cream or top of milk.

For sauce melt ½ oz butter in pan, add ½ oz flour and mix. To this add 1 gill of liquid (half milk, half macaroni stock). Stir, and boil for a few minutes.

Allow to cool slightly, then add 2 egg yolks, blending them in one at a time, ¼ teaspoon made mustard, 2 ozs grated cheese, pepper and salt to taste.

Whip 2 egg whites and, when stiff, fold in sauce.

Pour over macaroni, sprinkle a little Parmesan cheese on top and bake at 375° for about 30 minutes until slightly risen and golden brown.

Mrs Cruickshank,
Invermark Lodge

SCOTCH WOODCOCK

2 slices toast.
1 oz margarine.
1 hard-boiled egg.
Pinch of cayenne and white pepper.
1 dessertspoon anchovy essence.
Custard.
1 yolk of egg.
¼ pint milk.
Pepper and salt.
1 dessertspoon chopped parsley.

Chop egg, pound with the margarine and anchovy essence and work all together until quite smooth.

Sandwich this between the slices of hot buttered toast and cut into fingers.

Arrange these in a dish and keep hot.

Mix yolk and seasoning, add hot milk and strain into pan.

Add parsley and cook until it thickens without boiling, then pour the custard over the toast.

Mrs Forbes,
Woodhaugh.

SKIRLY

(Also known as Creashie Mealie or Rummelty Thump)

Melt 2 tablespoons dripping in a pan.
Cook a sliced onion until soft.
Stir in as much oatmeal as fat will take up. Season.
Cook slowly for ten minutes, adding either milk or water.
Allow 2 tablespoons oatmeal per person.
Skirly should be fairly dry in consistency.

Miss D. Skene,
Waterside.

In common with other country areas, the Glen used to have its own meal mills. The best local meal is said to have come from Mill of Aucheen. Older folk in the Glen will tell you that today's commercially produced oatmeal has lost much of its texture by over-refinement and cannot be compared with the locally ground oatmeal of yesteryear.

In many areas it has now certainly become very difficult to acquire pinhead oatmeal which is a great pity, as this particular type goes well in the making of haggis.

OATMEAL BALLS

1 teacup oatmeal.
1 teacup stale bread, soaked and wrung out of cold water.
2 ozs margarine.
½ teaspoon pepper.
½ teaspoon salt.
1 small onion, finely chopped.

Moisten mixture with cold water, keeping a fairly firm consistency.

Flour hands and form mixture into firm balls.

Place in stew and cook for half an hour.

These make an excellent accompaniment for stewed rabbit or hare.

Miss E. Davidson,
Migvie.

MENUS FOR CLIPPING DINNERS AND TEAS

The general aim in the planning of a clipping dinner is to provide good plain food and plenty of it.

TURNABRANE

DINNER

Scotch broth

Boiled beef

Milk pudding with stewed fruit

Tea

Bannocks and home-made cheese

TEATIME

Boiled ham

Potatoes or stovies

Scones

Pancakes

Bannocks and cheese

CAIRNCROSS

DINNER

Scotch broth

Brisket (10 lbs)

Rice pudding with stewed apples

Tea

Plain biscuits

TEATIME

Mince

Bread

Oatcakes

Scones

Pancakes

Gingerbread

Fruit cake

At one time Glentennet clippings were none too popular, as the dinner was invariably hard fish!

MOSS DINNERS

MILK BARLEY.—Boil barley in water, add milk and salt or sugar to taste.

STEEPIES.—Bread soaked in milk and sprinkled with sugar.

Flagon of soup.

The above are typical of a period of Glen life which has well and truly passed away.

When peat-cutting was in progress, everyone who was able lent a hand in the work. This included the womenfolk, who helped to stack the peat as it was cut. As always on a farm, there also remained the other daily chores, so at times like these the mid-day meal was geared to minimum time in preparation.

At these times, too, the meal was often taken out to the site in order to save time.

BEER and WINES

Southernwood or "Appleringie"

a one-time popular aromatic shrub
found in Glen gardens

" Cripple Dick upon a stick,
Sandy on a soo,
Gaed a the wey tae Aiberdeen
Tae buy a pund of 'oo."

BEER

The basic recipe requires the hops to be boiled and strained and added to sugar, malt, etc., which must be thoroughly dissolved to make sure that all the ingredients are well mixed.

Fermentation takes place in a temperature of 65° - 75°F. If room temperature is lower than this, there is a real risk of ceilings being decorated with patterns of beer gone mad, not to mention the shock to the nervous system of anyone unfortunate to open a bottle of such a brew.

It is advisable to skim the surface of the brew lightly 24 hours after fermentation has begun.

Fermentation has ceased when bubbles collect in a ring at the centre. Use this as the ultimate guide, rather than a number of days as laid down in the recipes, as conditions can vary slightly depending on the time of year.

Store in screw top bottles when ready.

Use yeast according to packet instructions.

LAGER

4½ lbs dried malt extract, 1 oz hops, 2 gallons water, yeast.

MILD BROWN ALE

5 ozs hops, 8 gallons water, 3 lbs brown sugar, 2 teaspoonfuls yeast.

BEER

Alcohol content ...	3%	5%	7%	9%
Gallons water ...	5	5	5	5
lbs sugar	3	4	5	6
lbs malt extract ...	1	2	3	4
Hops (ozs)	1	2	4-6	6-8
Days to clear	7	14	21	28
Keeps for	weeks	months		years

For dark beer use moist brown sugar in the above recipe and for a pale light-bodied beer use Demerara sugar. Syrup gives a still lighter colour but takes longer to clear. In stout, black treacle is substituted for the sugar.

P. Thomson.

PLUM PORT

Boil one gallon water and pour over 4 lbs damsons.
Leave for one day, then squeeze and crush damsons.
Stir daily for five days.
Strain through a muslin bag.
Stir in 4 lbs sugar and add one breakfastcup boiling water.
Leave to ferment for eight days, then skim and bottle.

Mrs H. Ferrier,
Cuttlehaugh.

ADVOCAAT

1 large tin Carnation milk.
3 lemons.
1 gill brandy.
3 eggs.
1 lb caster sugar.

Squeeze lemons, break in three eggs, including shells, in a large bowl.

Leave for three days, stirring frequently, then sieve out any shell left.

Add sugar and milk and whisk well.

Add brandy slowly, and fold in.

Bottle, and shake well before use.

Mrs H. Ferrier,
Cuttlehaugh.

APPLE WINE

24 lbs apples.
1 gallon water.
3 lbs sugar per gallon.
Yeast.

Chop apples into small pieces, place in bowl, and add yeast and water (This will not quite cover apples).

Leave for one week, stirring several times per day.

Keep pan closely covered in a warm place.

Strain juice from pulp and press juice from apples.

Cask, then rack when cleared.

This wine is ready to drink in six months.

P. Thomson.

DAMSON WINE

4 lbs damsons.
3 lbs sugar.
1 gallon water.
1 oz yeast.
1 slice toasted bread.

Cook damsons in water until tender.
Strain on to sugar, and stir until melted.
Leave until mixture is lukewarm.
Spread yeast on slice of toast and place on liquid.
Yeast and toast may be removed after 48 hours.
Strain and bottle. Cork lightly, and tighten when fermentation has ceased in 7 - 10 days.

Mrs H. Ferrier,
Cuttlehaugh.

ELDERBERRY GINGER WINE

1 gallon elderberries.
1 gallon water.
3½ *lbs sugar.*
1 oz whole ginger.

Strip berries from stems.
Add water, boil for 15 minutes, then strain, throwing pulp away.
Add sugar and stir until dissolved.
Ferment for 14 days, then skim and bottle.
Add the whole ginger, well bruised, when the wine is 6 months old, then keep for one month before using.

Mrs H. Ferrier,
Cuttlehaugh.

ELDERBERRY WINE

1 gallon elderberries.
1 gallon water.
3 lbs sugar.

Strip elderberries from stems, add water and boil for 15 minutes.

Strain, add sugar to the liquid and allow to ferment for 14 days, then skim and bottle and leave for 12 months.

Cork lightly at first.

Mrs H. Ferrier,
Cuttlehaugh.

ELDERBERRY PORT

2 quarts elderberries.
1 gallon water.
3 lbs sugar.
½ lb raisins.
1 oz yeast.

Strip berries from stalks, place berries in water, and boil for 15 minutes.

Strain, then add sugar and chopped raisins to liquid and simmer gently for 20 minutes.

Cool, add yeast spread on toast and leave to ferment for 14 days before skimming and bottling.

Cork lightly until fermentation has ceased, then cork firmly and keep for twelve months.

Mrs H. Ferrier,
Cuttlehaugh.

BIRCH WINE

1 gallon birch juice.
3 lbs preserving sugar.
1 lb raisins.
½ oz crude tartar.
1 oz almonds.

Pour the juice, sugar and raisins into pan.
Stir over low heat till sugar is dissolved.
Turn into a tub and add cream of tartar.
Allow to ferment 6-7 days.
Strain into flask, tie almonds in muslin bag and add to juice.
When fermentation ceases, remove bag and bung up cork.
Leave for five months, then fine and bottle.
Store bottles in a cool cellar.

(Birch juice is most easily tapped in the early part of spring, when the sap begins to rise).

Mrs W. Macdonald,
Birchgrove.